Frank Freeman's Dancing School

CLIFF YATES was born in Birmingham in 1952. He won both the Aldeburgh first collection prize and the Poetry Business book & pamphlet competition for *Henry's Clock* (Smith/Doorstop). During his time as Poetry Society poet-in-residence he wrote *Jumpstart Poetry in the Secondary School*. He teaches at Maharishi School, where his students are renowned for winning poetry competitions, and runs courses and workshops in Britain and abroad. He received a 2003 Arts Council England Writer's Award.

Also by Cliff Yates

POETRY
14 Ways of Listening to the Archers (Smith/Doorstop, 1994)
Henry's Clock (Smith/Doorstop, 1999)
Emergency Rations (Smith/Doorstop, 2004)

TEACHING
Jumpstart Poetry in the Secondary School (Poetry Society, 1999, 2004)

AS EDITOR
Oranges: Poems from Maharishi School (Maharishi School Press, 2001)

Frank Freeman's Dancing School

Cliff Yates

London

PUBLISHED BY SALT PUBLISHING
Fourth Floor, 2 Tavistock Place, Bloomsbury, London WC1H 9RA United Kingdom

All rights reserved

© Cliff Yates 2009

The right of Cliff Yates to be identified as the
author of this work has been asserted by him in accordance
with Section 77 of the Copyright, Designs and Patents Act 1988.

This book is in copyright. Subject to statutory exception
and to provisions of relevant collective licensing agreements,
no reproduction of any part may take place without the written
permission of Salt Publishing.

Salt Publishing 2009

Printed Great Britain by the MPG Books Group,
Bodmin and King's Lynn

Typeset in Swift 9.5 / 13

*This book is sold subject to the conditions that it shall not,
by way of trade or otherwise, be lent, re-sold, hired out,
or otherwise circulated without the publisher's prior consent
in any form of binding or cover other than that in which
it is published and without a similar condition including this
condition being imposed on the subsequent purchaser.*

ISBN 978 1 84471 503 9 paperback

Salt Publishing Ltd gratefully acknowledges
the financial assistance of Arts Council England

1 3 5 7 9 8 6 4 2

Contents

EMERGENCY RATIONS	1
Lighthouse	3
Locked In	4
Thank You for the Postcard I Read It	5
Emergency Rations are Tasting Better and Better	6
Fishing	8
He Squeezes Tennis Balls to Strengthen his Hands	9
On the Third Day	10
Leaves are Just Thin Wood	11
Summers	12
The Morning they Set Off it was Snowing	13
Daglingworth Blues	14
There are Mountains but I Can't See Them	15
Cross Country	16
Day Breaks as a Petrol Station	17
L'Hermitage and a Bird	18
Hôtel de l'Angleterre	19
Shoes	20
Would You Listen to the Safety Instructions Please	21
At the Smell of the Old Dog	22
Proportion	23
Apple Trees in a Gale	24
Baldwin Road	25
FRANK FREEMAN'S DANCING SCHOOL	27
New White Bike	29
Hair	30
Yes	31

Fun	32
Borneo	33
Your Limbs Bound and Mouth Full of Cloth	34
In the Mountains of Truth You Will Never Climb in Vain	35
Picking Up Speed	36
Kidderminster-on-Sea	37
Climbing the Tree to Pick Fruit he Fell and Lost	38
Wake Up	39
The Ruler of Planet X	40
Return	42
When She Got Back After Her Funeral	43
Gower Road	44
Mid-Gallop	45
10 Easy Pieces for Piano	46
Vienna	48
Guitarist	49
On Police Records	50
Rock Cross	51
Noise	52
Fireside Bookshop	53
Knowledge of this Sort Helps Keep Society Together	54
Still Alive	55
Satsang with Paul	56
The Muleteer in the Orange Shirt	57
Shape	58
Chinese New Year	59
The Poem	60
On the Street in Bratislava	61
Boggle Hole	62
Mirror	63

Fever	64
The Science of Predictive Astrology	65
Fall	66
I Am a Crab	67
Oxygen Tent	68
Snow	69
Chez Marianne	70

Acknowledgements

Acknowledgements are due to the following, where some of these poems first appeared: *Cake Magazine, erbacce, Gists and Piths, Great Works, Neon Highway, The North, Orbis, Pages, Smiths Knoll, Stand, The Slab, Stride Magazine, Sunk Island Review, Tears in the Fence, The Rialto, Writers' Awards 2003* (London: Arts Council England, 2003), *Emergency Rations* was published by Smith/Doorstop in 2004. Many of these poems have undergone revision and differ from those versions originally published.

I am grateful for an Arts Council England Writer's Award (2003).

Emergency Rations

Lighthouse

The lighthouse flickers at the end of the pier.
We watch it in our red pyjamas.
Actually neither of us are wearing red pyjamas
you're wearing my blue shirt.

The lighthouse flickers at the end of the pier.
It's the only thing we can be sure of.
Everything's uncertain
since you set alight my record collection.

I'm trying to work out an appropriate reaction,
rearranging things in my head to eliminate
all memory of the record collection.
The lighthouse flickers on and off

actually it doesn't, you point out, it just appears to.
You look amazing in my blue shirt.
I haven't words to describe how good you look
in the light from the lighthouse. Now you're here

now you're not. Maybe I should burn
something of yours, you suggest.
Your voice leaves me in the dark.
It doesn't sound like you when I can't see you.

Locked In

If there was a skylight I could see the stars
if there were no clouds.
If there was a window I'd smash it . . .

Hopeless. Switch the lights back on,
kick aside the cushions, spend ten minutes
with Colin's darts and the *Lock Up Your Daughters* poster.
Don't touch Derek's computer.

Spare light bulb in the microwave,
turn off the lights—red, blue, yellow.
Remember the trick with the dill pickle,
the kebab skewer and the mains socket. The fridge hums

then stops. Prop the door open for company
and have an inconclusive game of football
with Celia's inflatable globe
then break into Margaret's locker with a biro,

find the tea money in the Coffee Mate tin,
count it twice, put it back
and write out a new washing-up rota
for the next six months in her handwriting

leaving myself out. Play with the idea
of the fire extinguisher. At 5 a.m.,
feet up on the table,
close my eyes, wait for the caretaker.

Thank You for the Postcard I Read It

A bat in the bedroom we opened the curtains and windows
the sound of its wings it flew in spasms.

I can't believe the address we are staying on Horse Road.
There are donkeys on the hill they lowered their eyes

jerking their tails to discourage the flies.
The abbey's stone windows open the sky.

On the beach we found ammonites in black stone
two boys with fishing rods cast again and again.

Four days of sunshine then in Scarborough it rained.
We didn't go into the t-t-t-tower of t-t-t-t-terror

but watched two girls run out squealing and pale
chased by a boy in bandages with a chainsaw.

The castle had guides like mobile phones but bigger
you could touch the repeat button and make it stutter

we had Winston Churchill say bomb-bomb-bomb-bomb
and a woman from the BBC say Dicky Dickinson Dicky-Dick-Dick.

King John lived on the hill he built living quarters
he wasn't the villain of the films it was Richard his brother.

I said you've still got your earrings on
she said I know it's part of the plan.

Emergency Rations are Tasting Better and Better

It's eleven in the morning, sun coming through,
next door's lawnmower doing a lawnmower impression.

The dried apricots were a treat, with our backs
to the wind, smoking our pipes while the huskies slept.

Maybe the telephone will ring, or I'll write a poem
in which every line will sound like the last line.

This is paradise were we not intent on starving.

I turn on the radio, turn it off again,
find the pencil sharpener and sharpen both pencils.

Poor Smith is missing his mother, makes pot
after pot of tea, melting snow by the bucketful
and is careful with our precious matches.

Maybe I'll write a novel, a short one.

He gave the last of his chocolate to Hughes
who gobbled it and fell straight to sleep
while the kettle whistled and the huskies whined.

The postman's been. We didn't have any letters.

Today I chewed tea, it was surprisingly bitter.

We've been in this house eight years
and still haven't painted the woodwork.

My beard has been frozen for days.

I think I'll go out and buy a newspaper

*Most of all I'd like to shave, to smell soap
and the touch of a warm towel, to hear the radio
through the bathroom door*

find out what's happening in the world.

Fishing

Nothing will content them but the extremest limit of land.
— Herman Melville

I cast like he shows me but his new reel
breaks from the rod, flies like a potato
and plops into the murk of Hurcott Pool.
We lean, elbows on wall, squinting at the water.

He snatches the rod, takes hold of the line,
leans out and pulls hand over hand you can
barely hear a ripple. Until with a splash it appears,
a pendulum in the sunshine, a prize, inches
away from us.

We improvise depth charges from fireworks,
drop them into the pool, anticipate
the muted bang, bubbles, a thousand dead
fish shimmering on the surface.

History. Mr Mort is shouting at him
for firing pellets at Andy Gunn.
He stands slowly. Six foot two
he's been shaving since the first year.

Two years later he moved to Australia.

He Squeezes Tennis Balls to Strengthen his Hands

He's playing the double bass in his room.
He plays it like a cartoon.
Notes climb down and up the stairs.
The ceiling reverberates.

A problem only comes into focus
when you think about it.
I like what's out of focus, the figure
in the background, off-centre
or even out the picture but you know she's there
(and not necessarily because you were).

Branches grow out of her head like antlers
reaching for the light that breaks through the trees.
You didn't notice the trees?

He squeezes tennis balls to strengthen his hands.
There are tennis balls all over the house
you have to be careful on the stairs
especially in the dark.

(Noises from the shed.)

Anyone who goes to the trouble
of stealing our lawnmower can have it.
At a certain time of the night you're past caring.
I lie there waiting for that moment.

On the Third Day

For my twenty-first we did the Mumbles Run
a pint in every pub on the Mumbles Road
between Blackpill and Limeslade. Brains
is the local brew. We said it's easy to see why.

The limp evening drizzled over the city
sodden paper settled on the pavements.
No one was pretending apart from the statues
and we didn't recognise the statues.

Graham showed me, on an earlier occasion
the art of drinking beer. You don't swallow
so much, you pour it down. If you have to swallow
take really big gulps, much bigger than you think

The station was nearly empty, the last train
had left and he was on the platform opposite
crouched over but unable to call out
hesitating before that moment . . .

don't worry you won't drown. I could down a pint
in NINE gulps, Graham in FIVE and Tony in ONE

his heart beating inside a stranger's chest
his eyes gazing out from a stranger's face.
It was probably too late to save him
a dog barked in the distance.

Some people came late and joined us half-way.
I didn't realise you could do that.

Leaves are Just Thin Wood

No, I don't read French.
Do you have a translation?
I'm from Birmingham.
Let's go for a walk in the woods. It's raining.

Bring the billiard table.
I have the balls in my trouser pockets.
Can you manage?
Here, let me hold the door.

Yes I agree, the rain. Did I mention
the importance of parks in the black country?
It's not that interesting. Mind
the rosa rugosas, their thorns,
and the climber with the orange hips.

All the other woods are memories
preparing us for this one.

If I tell anyone she'll kill me.
No, really—a dart through the forehead.
Look at my hands—people call it stigmata
but really it's darts.

We quarrelled in the autumn.
We quarrelled about the milk.
In the morning she left, took the bed with her.

Summers

We snorkelled every evening
for four years I had a tanned back.
You can't eat out in Mexico.

Two men in a suit not the same suit.
The second suit hands over the money
as if you'd been doing it all your life.

I gave it to the pretty one, who smiled.
Excuse me did you order this? No
we only drink water do you have water?

Write this down do you have paper?
Thank you for allowing me to do this.
Hope you like the view we left in your kitchen.

Your dog brought us a present a blanket.
We threaded burnt rope through the eyelets.
Spent matches among the gravel.

Leave us your keys we'll look after them.
It was nothing but thank you for thanking us
next year we'll do it again.

The Morning they Set Off it was Snowing

My brother's on his own at the table next to ours
tucking into chicken and cheese.

*There were no birds in the sky, no ships in the harbour
apart from theirs the radios were silent.*

He's okay he says he can see everyone
from here. The perfect host, more
relaxed now it's over. Two pints of beer
eat as much as you want it'll only go to waste.

*I peeled an onion and the centre was brown
as a rotten apple and as sweet.
The horses trembled and sweated in the paddock
and the butter melting in spite of the temperature.*

*It was unbelievably cold. Jenkins was shivering
and there is no one more used to it.
The villagers lined the road but no one spoke.
The cattle stood like painted cattle.*

On the way home, me and Ruth go for a walk past
the old house with the chickens and cows.
Dad, she says and treads in a cow pat, scuffs it off
on the grass. It's where we came last time
but I don't tell her I wait for her to notice.

Daglingworth Blues

The Vietnamese pot-bellied pig looks up
but doesn't see, eyes hidden in folds of flesh
and can't be bothered with the apple we've thrown
as two motorbikes throttle past and, in the light
from the living room, the bats are out over David's lawn.

The book itself on the blockboard coffee table:
Gas and Oil Opportunities in Libya.
Black oozes from its pages, stains the new
rush carpet, heads for the door and Daglingworth
as tankers set out from Al-Khama,
the U.N. floods Montenegro with Deutschmarks
and somewhere in Zimbabwe the sound of glass.

The Vietnamese pot-bellied pig stares at its skin
its meat tough as carpet. The bees are asleep
not that we notice dismantling their hive
in the sleeping wood while in the neighbouring field
a fox leaves behind the day-old lamb's two hind legs.

There are Mountains but I Can't See Them

It's dark pass me a spike Mike, drive it in
by my foot, give me something to stand on tonight
we'll sleep like the dead Mike thankful
under whirling stars. Smith isn't looking
too good you have to keep an eye
on him like I do you. Is this clear? The mountain is
not clear it's under our feet but isn't this moving train.

Mike are you still there?
All that winter we dreamed strawberries.
Four months no sunlight, air colder than the freezer
when powdered eggs of all things saved us.

Tell us a joke Mike, one about the chickens.
Have a telephone ring, engineer
an interruption during the telling.
Have the door handle turn your cigarette
light of its own accord. Tell it tonight
at the foot of the mountain.

Time passed slowly in the forest
then we got up to go for a drink.
I forget the name of the pub.
At no point did I remember it.

Cross Country

Cross country and I'm stretched out
on the grass verge of Stourbridge Road
grinning at the sun like a holidaymaker.

We left the bulk of our equipment at last night's camp
no one speaks for hours as if speech is unfamiliar
I look forward to the nights, to sleep.

Lorries thunder past but no one's laughing
and then I see why. He stands on the hill, arms folded
like an Indian, whistle round neck, moccasins apart.

I fear we have reached that stage. The screen
between living and dying is thin cotton or paper
we see the snow through this screen and each other
it vibrates in the wind as if it will tear.

In the changing room he's the white man. The whistle swings.
Gary Cooper, John Wayne, the law in his hands.
He grabs my hair, jerks my head, slaps it once,
twice, three times. The room goes black, white, red.

I wait for it to stop and the sun shines through
as if behind cloud but the cold makes such an impression.
I must get up out of the darkness and walk.
I force myself to open my eyes and realise
that I have been walking and not stopped.

'You miserable specimen.' His rugby career
in tatters. The pump on his desk, the showers.

Day Breaks as a Petrol Station

Day breaks deliberate as a petrol station
newspapers and expensive flowers
but you're tired of vacuum-packed sandwiches
and sordid headlines.

On the 1507 out of Deansgate
she's reading *The Holy Sinner*
the dog opposite smiles
through its muzzle.
Coffee or maybe something's on fire
we do appear to be speeding
unless we're stationary and the landscape's
rattling past. 'It's been a good day.
It makes up for yesterday.'
'Why, what happened yesterday?'

Days without rain and suddenly it rains.
Another country, your body's not your own.
Breakfast in bed after so many days.
You want to go for a walk. In this?

L'Hermitage and a Bird

head back, a single drop of blood from its beak
on the concrete *like a red coin*. Dead eyes
white feathers. It flew into the window and life left it.

*I keep doing that. I'm covered in bruises
but amazingly still alive.*

>Vittel's autumn gold and red. Strange
>after the mountains, the pines, snow,
>the sky's unbelievable blue
>from the train crossing the border.

Drums, drums for the bird in flight.
A different sound when it hits the window.

Hôtel de l'Angleterre

No thanks I don't want a Sandwich Americana.
I'm turning yellow maybe it's the noodles.
I said what do you think should I start

feeling ill? She said my headache's enough
for both of us. I said what about
my toothache? She said what toothache?

Birds sing in French; *massage énergétique*
on a lamppost. What a city, what a language!
I have an owl sandwich, an owl shower.

Man on the Metro with one arm does a crossword
in a pink shirt, two men on crutches
in the same carriage. A convention perhaps.

Picasso knew some strange-looking people.
He's excited and she's looking pretty damn good as well.
Large nude in red armchair, large bather with book.

Two profiles for the price of one
and the hat's the only thing straight.
The hat's not straight.

A boy throws a small cardboard
box at a pigeon. What we need
here is a thousand-piece jigsaw.

Shoes

I grieve for them on the long winter evenings

First the hard brush for the mud. Let
the dust settle, then a dishcloth
dipped in the galvanised bucket
of rain water. So cold my fingers
would ache if I let them.

Jenkins with his clear blue eyes

They'll dry smeared so I drag
the brush through the blacking
like my dad showed me, not dab it
so it dries out, and brush into the leather
between the sole and the upper.

Smith with his indomitable spirit

Next the soft brush. Skim
lightly across till they shine. Like new
but not like new: Luke's shoes, size twelve.
An old towel to finish off.
See—he won't recognise them.

Jones with his laugh like a horse.

Would You Listen to the Safety Instructions Please

At thirty thousand feet he cradles three roses
in a bottle of water between his legs. She coughs.

He looks at her ear, rubs his cheek on her shoulder.
The yellow one's faded, the edges of its petals brown.

She puts his head in her lap, she puts her head
in his lap, he puts his head in her lap.

He loved the towering peaks of his native mountains.

They move right to left across the ceiling.

At the Smell of the Old Dog

the cat stares at the space
under the table we burn
a haystack of joss sticks
prop the sash with kindling.

It's no good if she's not happy
restless. Same dog
asleep on the same step
doesn't make any difference.

Telescope needs a coin
to see the boat bright sun.
Kids in wet suits jump. Boy
cradles a bottle of raspberryade.

Three girls arm in arm
wade chest deep across the bay
their voices carry.
They're on the hill maybe

a little cold and hungry.
You'd give a fortune
no. Something forgotten . . .
fishing boat, rope faded orange, blue.

Proportion

He was never off sick but the day
that he was, unfamiliar in faded pyjamas,
unbrushed hair, I climbed in with him
with a pencil and new sketchbook.

He showed me how to draw in proportion:
hold the pencil vertical at arm's length,
measure the distance with your thumb, mark it.
Now horizontal. We drew the window,

the bedroom window, the pattern
in stained glass, the shape of the flower,
the criss-crossed leading and then
we drew the sun coming through.

Apple Trees in a Gale

Under our feet the vast
roots take the strain, stand
out like veins beneath the turf.

She picks apples in her apron
piles them on the ground
while Dad unravels a rope
knocks in a stake.

I hold a branch's weight
against the wind as the sky cracks
and spills onto the garden.

Baldwin Road

Patches of melting snow on the sodden lawn
the other side of the coal bunker we built and demolished.
Horses shiver in the field. My dad cycles up the hill
on his way to work, haversack on his shoulder,
beret pulled low. It's his last day.
Next door but one the John Denver look-alike
is burying something in the garden, watched
by his new dog, ears back, tail moving.

Jack sweeps his drive, sweeps up the years,
gathers them in a bucket, leaves
them by the streetlight that's still on.
Condensation. A noise
from the chimney. The photographs
on the mantelpiece pull themselves together.

Frank Freeman's Dancing School

One of the most famous concerts on the [1968] tour was at the Sunday Club at Frank Freeman's Dancing School in Kidderminster. [John Peel] describes what took place: 'When I told them they said, 'Wow, it's a really groovy name.' I said, 'No, it's not a groovy name, it's a dancing school run by a bloke called Frank Freeman.'

— MIKE BARNES, *Captain Beefheart*

New White Bike

Cheyney Road, weaving through traffic
overtaking the queue at the lights.
Our car. The kids scream
with laughter when they see me.
Gill smiles. I bang on the window,
pull faces, pretend to fall off.

The big house, corner of Brook Lane
I'd love to live there. French windows
overlooking the garden. Now the hill.
I'll need a shower after this.

Across the playground, swerving
between groups of kids, heading
for 'B' block. A fifth year
opens the door. Along
the corridor, no hands. Two girls
step back. Into the staffroom,
once round the table, ringing
the bell. Margaret spills her tea.
Pete laughs, shakes his head.
Colin shouts, 'Yatesy!' and claps.
Derek's face . . .

Hair

A cow chomping grass outside the window
left open all night even the coldest. Fresh air
she said, brushing hers in the full-length mirror.
Her hair was shiny and probably still is.

As she brushed it got shinier. Where
would you rather be, she asked. I had no idea.
She assumed this was to do with happiness
but it wasn't, I just had no idea. By that time

there were two cows, you could hear their huffing
as well as grass tearing. They seemed hungry
but not desperate. I can't imagine a desperate cow.
Maybe that's a failure of nerve, she said,

turning towards me, for the son
at that moment had entered the room.
He had her eyes and was towelling his hair
tall and moist from the shower.

Yes

1.

I suppose it's good of them to come back
to Frank's, now that they're famous.
They're well into their set when he stands up
and accuses them of sitting on their laurels.

Jon Anderson stares, the bass player
stares and Jon Anderson says something.
I can't remember what he says. Then
they play 'Eleanor Rigby.' It's a fine moment.

2.

I can't remember how we got there
but there's the four of us:
him and his mate, me and my girlfriend
drinking pints of mild, eating crisps,

playing darts and he asks me if, later on,
would it be okay if I didn't think
of my girlfriend so much
as *my* girlfriend, so we could all

have a good time, all four of us.
He explains what a good idea
this is, if she's up for it. It sounds
perfectly reasonable, a good

outcome to the evening and in everyone's
best interests. I told him to get lost.

Fun

Al said he was glad that his girlfriend wasn't with him
when he watched *American Beauty*
he'd have been embarrassed.
We'd just got back from Paris.
Best bit was outside the bar, not being able to stop
laughing.

Such as when the telephone rings at one
in the morning, like it did last night,
and your neighbour's just chased your son
off his garden—his daughter's having a sleepover
and the scallywag climbed his wall
and pulled out the tent pegs

or hire a gipsy caravan in the Outer Hebrides
like the bank manager and his wife
('you'll pass somewhere you can wash on the Thursday')
who packed three carrier bags with baby wipes.

Borneo

He said he was shot down somewhere or other,
scrabbled around in the ocean, washed up
in Colombia. He flew his glider over the mountains,
bribed customs when they landed in Nigeria,
shared his collection of heads with her.

Feet up on the deckchair he read the *Wizard*
cover to cover while her mother brewed pot
after pot of strong China tea. They called him
the man who never grew old. Her mother
had another name for him

she wrote it with her finger
in the condensation on the bathroom tiles
lying in the bath while downstairs
he and her daughter shooed out
the cats, did it on the sofa.

Your Limbs Bound and Mouth Full of Cloth

When they say shout, snort vigorously,
stamp your feet, look enthusiastic:
give it your best, try to impress. Remember
your sterling work and the lonely camp fires
think of your mother and all that she did

and when they dangle you from the ceiling
think height, think mountains,
racing up the Herefordshire beacon
in thin air, skidding down in the cardboard box
that smells of apples.

Stand still while not standing still.
Sit up while climbing.
Lie down while not lying down.

Dream of knives and bullet-proof vests.
Your chest is a face, have you thought of that?
Looked at with this in mind, any landscape
becomes a friend.

The beach deserted except for an old crab. And I mean old.

In the Mountains of Truth You Will Never Climb in Vain

It's beyond the next peak your companion says
and the guide grins malevolently
though it might be a cultural barrier.
You watch him struggle with the tin-opener
as the fire crackles and spits at his face.

You force yourself awake to see what he's up to—
he's snoring like a buffalo under a mountain of blankets.
You'd happily sack him but he's indispensable
and that's what you pay him for, certainly not
for his cooking, looks or conversation.

And you wonder how come he understands so little
when he speaks nine languages, two European,
when you're sure he's responsible
for the barely decipherable ironic comments
in the margins of your *King Solomon's Mines*.

You dream he's in the director's chair,
sharpening his pencil with a scimitar.
You're about to audition for *The End of an Empire*.

Picking Up Speed

cruising through Hemel Hempstead

*Stevenson's foot swollen, will have to cut
off his boot. Sledges heavier than usual.*

wondering whether Christianity
has a future and what you had for dinner.

*Bent forward against the first wind, ice
in our beards and a hundred miles left.*

Did you find the road I mentioned?

*We look at the sky with renewed understanding
since Johnson's talk on the subject a fortnight behind us.*

Twenty-five minutes late past the brown horses,
the car breakers, the Ovaltine factory

Kidderminster-on-Sea

Travellers journey to the Seven Stars to witness
the equinox tide lap the plinth of Baxter's statue.
You can buy cockles on Coventry Street, fish
for eels off the Swan Centre, cast your net
in Castle Street and come up with a view
of the market: renovated clocks, gravy drowning...

Ricky robbed his old man's meter
to pay off a dealer in Telford there's a statue of him
somewhere. Joe got married, lived on Hurcott Road
until she hit him with the kitchen door. He moved out,
pretended he knew your mother in the flat
above the bus station they demolished before he found Jesus.

There are relics in St George's Park buried under the bench
overlooking the bowling green where we turned on
the tramps in our lunch hour. O where are you now Charlie
shouting in greeting the name that we gave you
a thousand miles from Poland, the only English you know.

Climbing the Tree to Pick Fruit he Fell and Lost

Climbing the tree to pick fruit he fell and lost
most of his hearing.

He shakes my hand, talks in Slovakian,
tapping his pockets, looking suspiciously
around him for us to be careful, in the market, of thieves.

We don't find any thieves we find a kilo of walnuts
for less than a pound but we can't eat a kilo of walnuts.

Four thousand crowns on the table, a bag of poppy seeds
in the kitchen and we don't know what to say or how to say it.
She draws a bath in her notebook and climbs in.

Wake Up

Wake up entirely, pack the sledges and set out.
Declare the end of the war and make preparations for a party.
Declare the end of the party and prepare for war.
Fight the war with abandon and neglect.
Burn the musical instruments.
Search for caterpillars on the allotment, remember
you no longer have an allotment.

Tame wild beasts with steely determination
and a big stick. Start a fire and tell stories around it,
sing songs in tired voices but happy. Check
for hidden microphones. Fall enchanted
into bed, change the bed
for something else. Swap all the music
for pigeons, set free the pigeons.

Lean back in your chair, massage tired feet
and carry on running. Run down the shop,
buy a pound of pears, run back, discover
they're not pears they're fire-lighters. Listen
to incidental sounds of the street and realise yes
it's music. Count the bricks in the trees, ducks
on the pond. Run out of fingers, count on your children's.

The Ruler of Planet X
(Joe 'Ginger' Ferguson, gun-runner, smuggler and adventurer, having escaped from a South American prison, hijacks rocket G209X and heads for the mysterious Planet X . . .)

Is that a spot of blood on the hand
so casually placed on your colleague's shoulder,
the man with shut eyes and finger
pointing at yes the inevitable sky.

Yellow eye, white lab coat—
merely a cipher at zero plus two—
looks briskly over his shoulder
as the hijacked rocket takes off.

Who cares who's in the saddle?
Who cares who's seeing
sweet Earth smaller and smaller
in the rear-view mirror?

Keep going. Planet X awaits
with her delicate blue-skinned children.
Just watch him go. Devil's speed.
Pass the dice Ronald, open your eyes . . .

~

Four horsemen in the beams
recoil. Whites of their eyes.
Mouths open, teeth bared, green hats
dislodged as the horses rear in terror. This

is what happens when you mess with history.
The anchor rips the boat in half.
Rowing down the road the fat man sweats,
the oars ragged from scraping tarmac.

Gaze at the boiling kettle, the modern
steam locomotive. The pillars of the temple
shift, the roof cracks and falls about their heads.
Who is G209X? Lost in the ink of space . . .

∼

By virtue of his shape, his bulk, his
language, the way his mouth
moves, his hands,

he knits himself a toga, lords it—
his every need—taller than them and stronger,
calculating brain, facial hair.

His sex life on the planet? impact
on the economy? technological
advancement before? after?

∼

Heading away from the blue-skinned planet,
ready to die in his own air . . .
behind him, a statue in his cast-off clothes
points to the horizon where neither sun sets.

He sleeps in the stern, curled like a foetus,
hands between knees, heading for a stranger planet,
a home he'll fail to recognise.
Sleep on a park bench. Break back into prison.

Return

He unzips his jacket, freeing first one head,
then the other. Three necks stretch this way
and that, eyes squint in the glow from the fire.

Rain hisses on the brazier. I pull up my hood,
take off my gloves, rub my hands together.
He looks at me. 'Why'd you come back?'

'Curiosity. Time for a change.'
Earth beckoned. A speck of dust
in the eye of the sky.

'Where are the others?' 'Early yet.'
They'll come with their bottles
and stories. There are no secrets here.

The noise of the city. Orange fog
across the waste. No clouds. Stars.
Kevin dreams of pond weed and fish

the hollow drumming of a heart
the sky through a few feet of water.

When She Got Back After Her Funeral

the bedroom light was on.
Who would have taken the trouble
and why? It had been a long day.
Her own funeral. All she wanted to do
was sleep, but she could never sleep
with the light on.

She puts her face to the window,
cupping her hands so she can see out:
Jack's garden, laid to lawn
but the auriculas he planted still coming up.

Her legs are tired, she can't remember
when they weren't, but her knees
feel her own for the first time in years.

She remembers hunger.
Streetlights from Bruce Road.
It's the lights that she'll miss, she decides
the corner shop with its tragic history

as melting snow thuds on the roof
the cries of the beleaguered traveller
echo from the mountain.

Gower Road

He dreams all day of a crowded party,
strangers dancing round his room
with the sink in the corner

and American
novels on the mantelpiece.
All he has to do is lie there

every possible future
at that moment before him.

Rain streams down an inside wall
loosening the plaster.
We gather downstairs in the sitting room

with the landlord's piano
then it's Saturday Night, the gateway
to Sunday Morning

by Velvet Underground and Nico
the one with the banana on the cover.

Mid-Gallop

Fried egg on toast, tea and chocolate biscuits
and a letter from a friend . . .
I don't know whether we had a good Christmas
but if I write about it I'll find out.

Today I drew a horse, a Chinese horse
in mid-gallop. Best thing I've done all week.
A complete accident

                    satisfying
like the chocolate biscuits, a bit of shading
or a line or two here and there
makes all the difference.

                        You go so far
then do something else, and suddenly
there's life in it.

10 Easy Pieces for Piano

❖

Everyone watches the child walk
through security and spread out her arms.
Today she'll fly. *You can always tell an Italian.*

❖

The Cuban landlady sings 'when you've had black
there's no going back.'
Her Slovakian cleaner has no papers.
We have an appointment, remember?

❖

My hearing went and my head exploded I've never had that
    before.
Remember Klaus? He sent a postcard, hey British how you
    doing.

❖

We missed the headlines on that day
man with backpack on CCTV.

❖

In Hintersee Gasthof the framed cartoon
the king, the farmer, the bishop, the worker
and top of the pyramid the man in black
'*Der Jude—er nimmt das Geld*'.

❖

Where does the roof end and the wall start?

❖

She said she found herself joining in
throwing flowers at Hitler. When he'd gone
she rushed into church, feeling
she'd slept with someone she shouldn't have.

❖

Anna went to collect her rabbit
'that's not my rabbit' she said.
He held it by the ears, back legs spread-eagled
and put his hand around its balls.

❖

This is my second favourite café in Vienna.

Vienna

what does
she see in him, the fat older man with the beard
as he looks at the menu the white table
she can't stop smiling   dark hair, interested eyes

   you look at your arm as it moves and think, mine?

this is east look at the architecture a Turkish church
they got this far
                we went quite far then came back:
windows, shutters open onto the street light and cool
cigarette butts in the ashtray, one on the window ledge

close to the mountains the drunken bed

   you are complete, happiness as you remember it

make love on the salty ground
lick the salt out of each other's wounds

       they fly in your face like birds

Guitarist

He didn't stop he carried on
didn't play by ear but learnt to read music
filed the frets so it sounded acoustic.

Didn't wake up with the rustle from his rucksack
didn't raise the broom handle and wait like an axe man
while we tipped the bag for the mouse to run.

Didn't miss and jar his wrists.
I didn't see him again. It wasn't him that time
across the bar in the Running Horse.

He didn't strip those wires
that night in his room
he wasn't there when they found him.

On Police Records

There are eyes in trees, the street's
a stage set, a set-up. They're in the wings
there are things said. Whispered.
Everyone's in on it.

We're down the Viaduct lunch time—
pint of shandy, cheese and onion.
The long walk back up the hill. We're on
police records. We're known. Our bones
show up on X-rays.

He throws a stick for the dog in Habberley Valley.
The tattoos fly from his arms, land in the bracken like leaves.

Rock Cross

Walking back in the immense dark
with the stars above us and the black trees
our ears ring and ring

and surrounded by distance and stillness
we shout in our heads at the top of our voices.

Noise

I don't remember twitching in my sleep
all I remember is waking up at 6.15
to the sound of the brook and a little
more light and remembering who
I am and where, and not stumbling
on the unfamiliar stairs.

We stood still and the noise stopped:
'It's my handbag, I always do that.
Sometimes I hear something and hold
my breath and the noise stops. Otherwise
how would I know? It could be frightening.'

We open the window and the brook
starts up, the birds flap their wings
and the wind comes into the room.
It circles the light bulb,
avoiding the corners, lightheaded,
confused at the absence of space.

Sometimes we forget to open the window and wonder
    why it's so quiet.

Fireside Bookshop

An Anthology of Chinese Poems. I read
half of it in the shop and again
overlooking the lake, sheltering the book
in my jacket from the rain.
The poems are different in the open air.

Back at the cottage we cook lunch,
onion gravy and mushrooms on new
potatoes. Fresh cherries and chocolate.

The brook through the open window.
It sounds like rain at home. Heavy rain
pouring down the downspout into the drain.
We heard it through the night.
Same brook, different water.

Knowledge of this Sort Helps Keep Society Together

she says, drawing a line with her lipstick
on the stationary car, smirking in the wing mirror
and eyeing the approaching clouds with trepidation
bordering on the kind of excitement she felt
discovering the pair of old cinema seats only
ten pounds each she bought for the greenhouse,
that faded all through the summer like old curtains
not made for sunlight.

Sometimes it's necessary to close the shutters
and pour a cool drink down the throat of the afternoon
that started so imaginatively, in a deprived
kind of way, unanticipated in spite of the white bird
ominously ascending into the clear sky overlooking
the harbour, boats bobbing below as boats bob
in memory, and such heat bearing down
almost too much to bear.

Still Alive

He's more or less on time. I notice him
across the road before he sees me.
His beard almost completely grey
and I'm surprised how short he is
which is nothing to do with age
I'd just forgotten. I said these are
new shoes but the grip is no good
a wet pavement like this is an ice-rink.
I notice my shoelace undone
and bend down to tie it in the busy street
he apologises to the couple behind
who have to step around me. I look
up. Here, you could tie this. He laughs.

Satsang with Paul

On Monday it's Liverpool which they're rebuilding.
The Egg Café is painted purple with yellow leaves.
We sit next to Chinese girls talking and laughing
and have veggie mince with rice it's exhausting.
There's a bike on the balcony against the railings
by the speakers. It's not raining but colder
than yesterday, the sun staying hidden.
Followed by cake and coffee one piece between us.

On the staircase there are posters for yoga
and acupuncture and *Poetry & Music*
at the Pilgrim where I once did a reading
to an audience of ten and the barman
and one for *Satsang with Paul,* helping you
experience the bliss of your inner being.

The Muleteer in the Orange Shirt

laughs into his drink, swallows it down, wipes his moustache with the back of his hand, looks across the table at the visitors and sizes up the width of their shoulders and wrestling prowess, their ability to wive and raise cattle, their expertise with weaponry and defence against knives, their amazement at unfamiliar landscapes, ability to handle boats in alternative weather, habits with horses and sheep, aptitude for scurvy and yellow fever, skill with alcohol and bizarre eating habits. Visitors who land periodically in unworthy vessels bringing concealed weapons, untreatable diseases and strange seeds which grow into stranger plants, crops that consume the land and drink the rain.

Shape

Thunder after a restless night, rain splashes
in the courtyard. The workmen will be back
in September. In the apartment opposite
a girl climbs a stepladder and paints the ceiling.

A motorcyclist pulls in by Café Columbus,
buys an ice-cream in the shape of a rose.
Emerging from her sleeping bag on a park bench
next to a wheelchair, an old woman gazes

into a mirror.
The overgrown theatre is closed for the summer.
Footsteps on the stairs . . .
                            when they wash up
you can hear every glass in the water.

Chinese New Year

Silent as an aquarium
the queue on the staircase
moonwalk on glass

The umbrella spins
delicate white hands
carve space out of air

Birds fly in and out
of the wall
Waves lap the coast road

A man in a corridor
shakes the sea water
from his hands

The Poem

No pen, or paper—for each word
as it comes, I drop a leaf
into a bowl.
Then go on my travels.

All kinds of things happen
sometimes I think of the poem, but when I get back
I have just leaves, barely a bowlful.

I tip them onto the table, arrange them,
looking for the poem.
Nothing. I keep trying. Hours pass.
It rains. It stops raining. I barely notice.

I open the back door, scatter them
onto the path
let them land where they will.

On the Street in Bratislava

Fresh damsons on the trees on the roadside
that we pick in the sunshine, dust
on our sleeves and eat. Delicious
after all that cabbage. 'I read philosophy

too,' and she shows me the book by her bed.
Nearly dark, and the swallows dart
while they can about the white roof
the balcony overlooks. It's that kind of world.

The dead man's song is played everywhere
in the pre-revolutionary building. Such high
ceilings. Doors slam if you leave them

and the courtyard is full of rumour and smoke.
'We could not stand near the window
or open the curtains for fear of being shot.'

Boggle Hole

Two new mountain bikes chained to the fence,
three horses lean over, bite at the tyres,
get the chain between their teeth,
eat most of a saddle and a handlebar grip.

Boggle Hole Youth Hostel and someone
has written 'welcome to BOGGLE HELL'
on the bottom of the bunk above this one
in red felt tip and shaky writing.

A gang of hikers come in late—a bottle
smashes outside the door then it's quiet
but for the talking, distorted, muffled
through the wall, apart from that voice . . .

After breakfast a tractor tows a boat
named *Freedom* into the sea. There used to be
smugglers here and someone wrote 'LULU'
four feet high in the slipway's wet concrete.

Freedom is oil-grey, just below the horizon
when a dog tears along sideways, its tongue out,
tasting the salt on the wind, and, in the first
drops of rain, a boy draws a donkey in the sand.

Mirror

They bandage his ankle tight for the swelling.
He spends most of the night unravelling it
then, exhausted, sleeps through the day . . .

I gaze at the place where the eyes would be
listen to the words that come out of the skin
that's there in place of the hole for a mouth
in place of lips that open and close
and listen and listen to the words that form
in the empty air in front of the face
that's not really a face at all

Someone's written 'MIRROR' on a sheet of A4
in place of the mirror on the bathroom wall.

Fever

It's so long since you came here
the house and garden have changed position
the trees you won't believe are everywhere...

I wake up wet with sweat, terrified
of looking in the mirror. Stretched
so taut that you can see through my skin,
trying to get used to this body, I can only move

slowly. Twenty minutes to get dressed.
The day settles into a headache
that's not going to disappear no matter
how long I lie here. Where is this going?

As if drowning, my whole past before me,
I could see, for the first time, where
I'd gone wrong and I decided to apologise
to a number of people (you among them).
From now on things will be different...

I'm going to waste today. I'm going to do
nothing of any importance. Nothing important
is going to happen. Things are looking up.

Suddenly a blue sky and an aeroplane
through the window. And the trees are still standing.
I don't care about any of it.
Colour of her hair; colour of the blanket.
Go on—ask me *anything*.

The Science of Predictive Astrology

I'm Scorpio with Mars in the tenth
and some other configuration that means
according to one source (though it could be
the translation) death by weapon or fire.

But we don't take these things seriously,
flames crackling in the distance, arrows
falling from the sky; pretty much as usual
for this time of the morning, we're out
of milk, the yogurt past its sell-by
and the phone stopped ringing just as I got there.

It was probably my brother
with news of how many badgers
he saw last night. The night before
it was seven. 'Bring your own'
he said to his wife when she reached
for his binoculars. He was joking
but there's nothing funny about fire.

Fall

The tablets work but send him to sleep
though when he can make it, the eight inch reflector
is manoeuvrable, so that's a blessing,
what with the dodgy hip and that hill of a garden

and bearing in mind that time observing Mars,
when he stepped back off the low stone wall
at three in the morning and lay sprawled
on the rockery and January frost
calling softly for help while the guinea-pigs
trembled in the corner of their hutch

or after the Beer Festival, when he opened
the door pulling into Southampton, stepped off
the train before it stopped, fell and rolled on his back
after insisting that all the commemorative
glasses go in his rucksack because
he's the mature student, he's the sensible one.

I Am a Crab

I walk sideways across the beach. Right now
I'm trying to get out of the sun. It's hot
hotter than Mexico. I've never been to Mexico

but my grandfather has. I never met him
but I know he lived in Mexico.
I like to think he survived Acapulco

where divers dive off the cliffs
into the clear blue sea
but whether he did is a mystery.

He may not have heard of Acapulco.
He may not have seen that Elvis movie.

I'm not sleeping. I wake in a sweat,
go downstairs, switch off the burglar alarm,
drink milk from the fridge. Still alive.

Oxygen Tent

November. Wet November.
Handsworth, Birmingham.
She was in another room,
waiting. Five days.

All I know is that lungs are as big . . .

Room breath. Breathe room.
Glass. Mist. Walls. Outside,
November wet and wind.
Trees in the wind. Trees?

I am learning to breathe.

Snow

This morning on the Pennines, the snow,
as if through a tunnel, opening out, snow
on the bonnet too, blowing up, spraying
the windscreen.

        It did this once before
on the M5, Birmingham. We were
passing through, around Christmas,
everyone in the car, on the way home.
The blow of the heater, the click of the wipers

        and all you wanted to do
was look at the snow and say look,
look at the snow, look at it.

Chez Marianne

In the next apartment the children are quieter,
soon they'll run a bath and one of them
will lie in it, moving. She comes out
of the bathroom, her hair standing
shaped to a point like an alien.
Are you cold? No, I'm airing the towels.
That's a good idea, here, which
of these switches switches the light on?

The sun comes out as if by invitation.
Step any further back and you'll fall off
the edge Madame. I've seen this before in Spain:
her lips aren't moving but the words keep coming.

Outside Chez Marianne on Rue des Rosiers
a beggar begs from a big man with loose hair
and fly undone who smiles like Tommy Cooper
then walks in the opposite direction
and suddenly, down a side road, the full moon;
the traffic's too busy to stand here and admire it
though on the Seine it's reflecting in the water as well,
so they have two moons to admire, not one.